THE BIG BOOK OF

THOMAS CARLYLE

QUOTES

Curated by M.K.

"Teach a parrot the terms 'supply and demand' and you've got an economist."

"He who has health, has hope; and he who has hope, has everything."

"Long stormy spring-time, wet contentious April, winter chilling the lap of very May; but at length the season of summer does come."

"No man lives without jostling and being jostled; in all ways he has to elbow himself through the world, giving and receiving offence."

"Endurance is patience concentrated."

"I've got a great ambition to die of exhaustion rather than boredom."

"Nature alone is antique, and the oldest art a mushroom."

"A strong mind always hopes, and has always cause to hope."

"A loving heart is the beginning of all knowledge."

"Of all acts of man repentance is the most divine. The greatest of all faults is to be conscious of none."

"These Arabs, the man Mahomet, and that one century, - is it not as if a spark had fallen, one spark, on a world of what proves explosive powder, blazes heaven-high from Delhi to Granada! I said, the Great man was always as lightning out of Heaven; the rest of men waited for him like fuel, and then they too would flame."

"Foolish men imagine that because judgment for an evil thing is delayed, there is no justice; but only accident here below. Judgment for an evil thing is many times delayed some day or two, some century or two, but it is sure as life, it is sure as death."

"War is a quarrel between two thieves too cowardly to fight their own battle."

"When we can drain the Ocean into mill-ponds, and bottle up the Force of Gravity, to be sold by retail, in gas jars; then may we hope to comprehend the infinitudes of man's soul under formulas of Profit and Loss; and rule over this too, as over a patent engine, by checks, and valves, and balances."

"No pressure, no diamonds."

"Superstition! that horrid incubus which dwelt in darkness, shunning the light, with all its racks, and poison chalices, and foul sleeping draughts, is passing away without return. Religion cannot pass away. The burning of a little straw may hide the stars of the sky; but the stars are there and will reappear."

"Egotism is the source and summary of all faults and miseries."

"We have our little theory on all human and divine things. Poetry, the workings of genius itself, which, in all times, with one or another meaning, has been called Inspiration, and held to be mysterious and inscrutable, is no longer without its scientific exposition. The building of the lofty rhyme is like any other masonry or bricklaying: we have theories of its rise, height, decline and fall - which latter, it would seem, is now near, among all people."

"A man lives by believing something: not by debating and arguing about many things."

"Man is a tool-using animal. Without tools he is nothing, with tools he is all."

"Quackery gives birth to nothing;
gives death to all things."

"Do not be embarrassed by your mistakes. Nothing can teach us better than our understanding of them. This is one of the best ways of self-education."

"Silence is as deep as eternity,
speech a shallow as time."

"Show me the man you honor, and I will know what kind of man you are."

"If you look deep enough you will see music; the heart of nature being everywhere music."

"Everywhere in life, the true question is not what we gain, but what we do."

"The real use of gunpowder is to make all men tall."

"Experience is the best of school masters, only the school fees are heavy."

"Necessity dispenseth with decorum."

"Speech is silver, silence is golden."

"Isolation is the sum total of wretchedness to a man."

"The eye sees what it brings the
power to see."

"Every noble work is at first impossible."

"He who has no vision of eternity
has no hold on time."

"The mystical bond of brotherhood makes all men brothers."

"Weak eyes are fondest of glittering objects."

"Permanence, perseverance and persistence in spite of all obstacle s, discouragement s, and impossibilities: It is this, that in all things distinguishes the strong soul from the weak."

"Laughter is the cipher key wherewith we decipher the whole man."

"A vein of poetry exists in the hearts of all men."

"Music is well said to be the speech of angels."

"It is a strange trade that of advocacy. Your intellect, your highest heavenly gift is hung up in the shop window like a loaded pistol for sale."

"Who is it that loves me and will love me forever with an affection which no chance, no misery, no crime of mine can do away? It is you, my mother."

"If Jesus Christ were to come today, people would not even crucify him. They would ask him to dinner, and hear what he had to say, and make fun of it."

"The block of granite which was an obstacle in the pathway of the weak, became a stepping-stone in the pathway of the strong."

"No great man lives in vain. The history of the world is but the biography of great men."

"I do not believe in the collective wisdom of individual ignorance."

"Laughter is one of the very privileges of reason, being confined to the human species."

"Every day that is born into the
world comes like a burst of music
and rings the whole day through,
and you make of it a dance, a dirge,
or a life march, as you will."

"True friends, like ivy and the wall
Both stand together, and together
fall."

"Silence, the great Empire of Silence: higher than all stars; deeper than the Kingdom of Death! It alone is great; all else is small."

"Instead of saying that man is the creature of circumstance, it would be nearer the mark to say that man is the architect of circumstance. It is character which builds an existence out of circumstance. From the same materials one man builds palaces, another hovels; one warehouses, another villas; bricks and mortar are mortar and bricks until the architect can make them something else."

"A man willing to work, and unable to find work, is perhaps the saddest sight that fortune's inequality exhibits under this sun."

"What we become depends on what we read after all of the professors have finished with us. The greatest university of all is a collection of books."

"The three great elements of modern civilization, Gun powder, Printing, and the Protestant religion."

"Our grand business undoubtedly is, not to see what lies dimly at a distance, but to do what lies clearly at hand."

"Under all speech that is good for anything there lies a silence that is better, Silence is deep as Eternity; speech is shallow as Time."

"There are good and bad times, but our mood changes more often than our fortune."

"Popular opinion is the greatest lie in the world."

"Every new opinion, at its starting, is precisely in a minority of one."

"A person who is gifted sees the essential point and leaves the rest as surplus."

"Nothing is more terrible than activity without insight."

"We were wise indeed, could we discern truly the signs of our own time; and by knowledge of its wants and advantages, wisely adjust our own position in it. Let us, instead of gazing idly into the obscure distance, look calmly around us, for a little, on the perplexed scene where we stand. Perhaps, on a more serious inspection, something of its perplexity will disappear, some of its distinctive characters and deeper tendencies more clearly reveal themselves; whereby our own relations to it, our own true aims and endeavors in it, may also become clearer."

"Whatsoever thy hand findeth to do, do that with all thy might and leave the issues calmly to God."

"Without kindness there can be no true joy."

"Literature is the thought of thinking souls."

"The true university of these days is a collection of books."

"Talk that does not end in any kind of action is better suppressed altogether."

"A laugh, to be joyous, must flow from a joyous heart, for without kindness, there can be no true joy."

"The first duty of man is to conquer fear; he must get rid of it, he cannot act till then."

"The best lesson which we get from the tragedy of Karbala is that Husain and his companions were rigid believers in God. They illustrated that the numerical superiority does not count when it comes to the truth and the falsehood. The victory of Husain, despite his minority, marvels me!"

"Man is emphatically a proselytizing creature."

"Hero-worship exists, has existed, and will forever exist, universally, among mankind."

"Parliament will train you to talk; and above all things to hear, with patience, unlimited quantities of foolish talk."

"If you do not wish a man to do a thing, you had better get him to talk about it; for the more men talk, the more likely they are to do nothing else."

"Do the duty which lies nearest to you, the second duty will then become clearer."

"Make yourself an honest man, and then you may be sure there is one less rascal in the world."

"He that can work is born to be king of something."

"One monster there is in the world,
the idle man."

"Not what you possess but what you do with what you have, determines your true worth."

"Laissez-faire, supply and demand-one begins to be weary of all that. Leave all to egotism, to ravenous greed of money, of pleasure, of applause-it is the gospel of despair."

"It is through symbols that man consciously or unconsciously lives, works and has his being."

"With respect to duels, indeed, I have my own ideas. Few things in this so surprising world strike me with more surprise. Two little visual spectra of men, hovering with insecure enough cohesion in the midst of the unfathomable, and to dissolve therein, at any rate, very soon, make pause at the distance of twelve paces asunder; whirl around, and simultaneously by the cunningest mechanism, explode one another into dissolution; and, offhand, become air, and non-extant-the little spitfires!"

"Instead of saying that man is the creature of circumstance, it would be nearer the mark to say that man is the architect of circumstance."

"Not on morality, but on cookery, let us build our stronghold: there brandishing our frying-pan, as censer, let us offer sweet incense to the Devil, and live at ease on the fat things he has provided for his elect!"

"That a Parliament, especially a Parliament with Newspaper Reporters firmly established in it, is an entity which by its very nature cannot do work, but can do talk only."

"In a symbol there is concealment and yet revelation: here therefore, by silence and by speech acting together, comes a double significance. In the symbol proper, what we can call a symbol, there is ever, more or less distinctly and directly, some embodiment and revelation of the Infinite; the Infinite is made to blend itself with the Finite, to stand visible, and as it were, attainable there. By symbols, accordingly, is man guided and commanded, made happy, made wretched."

"Speak not at all, in any wise, till you have somewhat to speak; care not for the reward of your speaking, but simply and with undivided mind for the truth of your speaking."

"As there is no danger of our becoming, any of us, Mahometans (i. e. Muslim), I mean to say all the good of him I justly can."

"It were a real increase of human happiness, could all young men from the age of nineteen be covered under barrels, or rendered otherwise invisible; and there left to follow their lawful studies and callings, till they emerged, sadder and wiser, at the age of twenty-five."

"Speech is great, but silence is greater."

"Silence is the element in which great things fashion themselves together."

"Adversity is the diamond dust
Heaven polishes its jewels with."

"Nothing builds self-esteem and self-confidence like accomplishment."

"Nothing stops the man who desires to achieve. Every obstacle is simply a course to develop his achievement muscle. It's a strengthening of his powers of accomplishment."

"Silence is more eloquent than words."

"No iron chain, or outward force of any kind, can ever compel the soul of a person to believe or to disbelieve."

"When the oak is felled the whole forest echoes with it fall, but a hundred acorns are sown in silence by an unnoticed breeze."

"Conviction is worthless unless it is converted into conduct."

"A man without a goal is like a ship without a rudder."

"Imperfection clings to a person, and if they wait till they are brushed off entirely, they would spin for ever on their axis, advancing nowhere."

"All human souls, never so bedarkened, love light; light once kindled spreads till all is luminous."

"The most unhappy of all men is the man who cannot tell what he is going to do, who has got no work cut-out for him in the world, and does not go into it. For work is the grand cure of all the maladies and miseries that ever beset mankind,honest work, which you intend getting done."

"The beginning of all wisdom is to look fixedly on clothes, or even with armed eyesight, till they become transparent."

"The soul gives unity to what it looks at with love."

"If a man was great while living, he becomes tenfold greater when dead."

"To be true is manly, chivalrous, Christian; to be false is mean, cowardly, devilish."

"Wise man was he who counselled that speculation should have free course, and look fearlessly towards all the thirty-two points of the compass, whithersoever and howsoever it listed."

"Great is wisdom; infinite is the value of wisdom. It cannot be exaggerated; it is the highest achievement of man."

"If there be no enemy there's no fight. If no fight, no victory and if no victory there is no crown."

"The spiritual is the parent of the practical."

"It is the first of all problems for a man to find out what kind of work he is to do in this universe."

"The lies (Western slander) which well-meaning zeal has heaped round this man (Muhammad) are disgraceful to ourselves only."

"It is a mathematical fact that the casting of this pebble from my hand alters the centre of gravity of the universe."

"Today is not yesterday: we ourselves change; how can our works and thoughts, if they are always to be the fittest, continue always the same? Change, indeed is painful; yet ever needful; and if memory have its force and worth, so also has hope."

"Wondrous is the strength of cheerfulness, and its power of endurance - the cheerful man will do more in the same time, will do it; better, will preserve it longer, than the sad or sullen."

"Blessed is he who has found his work; let him ask no other blessedness."

"The devil has his elect."

"Acorns are planted silently by some unnoticed breeze."

"To believe practically that the poor and luckless are here only as a nusiance to be abraded and abated, and in some permissable manner made away with, and swept out of sight, is not an amiable faith."

"In every phenomenon the beginning remains always the most notable moment."

"Let each become all that he was
created capable of being."

"Youth is to all the glad season of life; but often only by what it hopes, not by what it attains, or what it escapes."

"True humor springs not more from the head than from the heart. It is not contempt; its essence is love. It issues not in laughter, but in still smiles, which lie far deeper."

"May blessings be upon the head of Cadmus, the Phoenicians, or whoever it was that invented books."

"Of all the paths a man could strike into, there is, at any given moment, a best path . A thing which, here and now, it were of all things wisest for him to do . To find this path, and walk in it, is the one thing needful for him."

"War is a quarrel between two thieves too cowardly to fight their own battle; therefore they take boys from one village and another village, stick them into uniforms, equip them with guns, and let them loose like wild beasts against one other."

"Secrecy is the element of all
goodness; even virtue, even beauty
is mysterious."

"The man of life upright has a guiltless heart, free from all dishonest deeds or thought of vanity."

"A stammering man is never a worthless one. Physiology can tell you why. It is an excess of sensibility to the presence of his fellow creature, that makes him stammer."

"There can be no acting or doing of any kind till it be recognized that there is a thing to be done; the thing once recognized, doing in a thousand shapes becomes possible."

"Work is the grand cure of all the maladies and miseries that ever beset mankind."

"For the superior morality, of which we hear so much, we too would desire to be thankful: at the same time, it were but blindness to deny that this superior morality is properly rather an inferior criminality, produced not by greater love of Virtue, but by greater perfection of Police; and of that far subtler and stronger Police, called Public Opinion."

"A person with a clear purpose will make progress, even on the roughest road. A person with no purpose will make no progress, even on the smoothest road."

"Thirty millions, mostly fools."

"The end of man is action."

"Heroes have gone out; quacks have come in; the reign of quacks has not ended with the nineteenth century. The sceptre is held with a firmer grasp; the empire has a wider boundary. We are all the slaves of quackery in one shape or another. Indeed, one portion of our being is always playing the successful quack to the other."

"You can make even a parrot into a learned political economist - all he must learn are the two words "supply" and "demand. "."

"A lie should be trampled on and extinguished wherever found. I am for fumigating the atmosphere when I suspect that falsehood, like pestilence, breathes around me."

"Silence is the eternal duty of man."

"See deep enough, and you see musically."

"Why did not somebody teach me the constellations, and make me at home in the starry heavens, which are always overhead, and which I don't half know to this day?"

"Once the mind has been expanded
by a big idea, it will never go back
to its original state."

"In idleness there is a perpetual despair."

"The coldest word was once a glowing new metaphor."

"Cherish what is dearest while you have it near you, and wait not till it is far away. Blind and deaf that we are; oh, think, if thou yet love anybody living, wait not till death sweep down the paltry little dust clouds and dissonances of the moment, and all be made at last so mournfully clear and beautiful, when it is too late."

"Providence has given to the French the empire of the land, to the English that of the sea, to the Germans that of-the air!"

"The depth of our despair measures
what capability and height of claim
we have to hope."

"A great man shows his greatness by the way he treats little men."

"What is all Knowledge too but recorded Experience, and a product of History; of which, therefore, Reasoning and Belief, no less than Action and Passion, are essential materials?"

"History is the essence of innumerable biographies."

"That great mystery of TIME, were there no other; the illimitable, silent, never-resting thing called Time, rolling, rushing on, swift, silent, like an all-embracing ocean tide, on which we and all the Universe swim like exhalations, like apparitions which are, and then are not: this is forever very literally a miracle; a thing to strike us dumb,-for we have no word to speak about it."

"Tell a person they are brave and you help them become so."

"Heroism is the divine relation which, in all times, unites a great man to other men."

"Let him who gropes painfully in darkness or uncertain light, and prays vehemently that the dawn may ripen into day, lay this precept well to heart: "Do the duty which lies nearest to thee," which thou know to be a duty! Thy second duty will already have become clearer."

"Violence does even justice unjustly."

"A well-written life is almost as rare as a well-spent one."

"It is the heart always that sees,
before the head can see."

"History shows that the majority of people that have done anything great have passed their youth in seclusion."

"For all right judgment of any man or things it is useful, nay, essential, to see his good qualities before pronouncing on his bad."

"Sarcasm I now see to be, in general, the language of the devil; for which reason I have long since as good as renounced it."

"The merit of originality is not novelty; it is sincerity."

"Old age is not a matter for sorrow. It is matter for thanks if we have left our work done behind us."

"In books lies the soul fo the whole past time."

"What you see, but can't see over is as good as infinite."

"Everywhere the human soul stands between a hemisphere of light and another of darkness on the confines of two everlasting empires, - Necessity and Free Will."

"One must verify or expel his doubts, and convert them into the certainty of Yes or NO."

"Woe to him that claims obedience when it is not due; woe to him that refuses it when it is."

"Worship is transcendent wonder."

"The old cathedrals are good, but the great blue dome that hangs over everything is better."

"Doubt, of whatever kind, can be ended by action alone."

"All that mankind has done, thought or been: it is lying as in magic preservation in the pages of books."

"We call it a Society; and go about professing openly the totalest separation, isolation. Our life is not a mutual helpfulness; but rather, cloaked under due laws-of-war, named fair competition and so forth, it is a mutual hostility."

"Music is well said to be the speech of angels; in fact, nothing among the utterances allowed to man is felt to be so divine. It brings us near to the infinite."

"Universal history, the history of what man has accomplished in this world, is at bottom the History of the Great Men who have worked here."

"Silence is the element in which great things fashion themselves together; that at length they may emerge, full-formed and majestic, into the daylight of Life, which they are thenceforth to rule."

"Stop a moment, cease your work, and look around you."

"Contented saturnine human figures, a dozen or so of them, sitting around a large long table. Perfect equality is to be the rule; no rising or notice taken when anybody enters or leaves. Let the entering man take his place and pipe, without obligatory remarks; if he cannot smoke. let him at least affect to do so, and not ruffle the established stream of things."

"Self-contemplation is infallibly the symptom of disease."

"Obedience is our universal duty and destiny; wherein whoso will not bend must break; too early and too thoroughly we cannot be trained to know that "would," in this world of ours, is a mere zero to "should," and for most part as the smallest of fractions even to "shall."

"Creation is great, and cannot be understood."

"History is a mighty dramos, enacted upon the theatre of times, with suns for lamps and eternity for a background."

"The dust of controversy is merely the falsehood flying off."

"Let one who wants to move and convince others, first be convinced and moved themselves. If a person speaks with genuine earnestness the thoughts, the emotion and the actual condition of their own heart, others will listen because we all are knit together by the tie of sympathy."

"It is part of my creed that the only poetry is history, could we tell it right."

"Every man has a coward and hero
in his soul."

"The great silent man! Looking round on the noisy inanity of the world,-words with little meaning, actions with little worth,-one loves to reflect on the great Empire of Silence."

"Caution is the lower story of prudence."

"There is in man a higher than love of happiness; he can do without happiness, and instead thereof find blessedness."

"Produce, produce! Were it but the pitifulest, infinitesimal fraction of a product, produce it in God's name. 'Tis the utmost thou hast in thee? Out with it then! Up, up! Whatsoever thy hand findeth to do, do it with thy whole might."

"Man, it is not thy works, which are mortal, infinitely little, and the greatest no greater than the least, but only the spirit thou workest in, that can have worth or continuance."

"Thou fool! Nature alone is antique, and the oldest art a mushroom; that idle crag thou sittest on is six thousand years of age."

"Every poet, be his outward lot what it may, finds himself born in the midst of prose; h e has to struggle from the littleness and obstruction of an actual world into the freedom and infinitude of an ideal."

"Is not light grander than fire?"

"I too acknowledge the all-out omnipotence of early culture and nature; hereby we have either a doddered dwarf-bush, or a high-towering, wide-shadowing tree! either a sick yellow cabbage, or an edible luxuriant green one. Of a truth, it is the duty of all men, especially of all philosophers, to note down with accuracy the characteristic circumstances of their education,-what furthered, what hindered, what in any way modified it."

"The latest gospel in this world is,
know thy work and do it."

"Man is a tool-using animal."

"Terror itself, when once grown transcendental, becomes a kind of courage; as frost sufficiently intense, according to the poet Milton, will burn."

"The first duty of man is that of subduing fear."

"All true work is sacred. In all true work, were it but true hand work, there is something of divineness. Labor, wide as the earth, has its summit in Heaven."

"The Orator persuades and carries all with him, he knows not how; the Rhetorician can prove that he ought to have persuaded and carried all with him."

"All deep things are song. It seems somehow the very central essence of us, song; as if all the rest were but wrappages and hulls!"

"All greatness is unconscious, or it is little and naught."

"To me the Universe was all void of Life, of Purpose, of Volition, even of Hostility; it was one huge, dead, immeasurable Steam-engine, rolling on, in its dead indifference, to grind me limb from limb. Oh vast gloomy, solitary Golgotha, and Mill of Death! Why was the living banished thither companionless, conscious? Why, if there is no Devil; nay, unless the Devil is your God?"

"The weakest living creature, by concentrating his powers on a single object, can accomplish something. The strongest, by dispensing his over many, may fail to accomplish anything. The drop, by continually falling, bores its passage through the hardest rock. The hasty torrent rushes over it with hideous uproar, and leaves no trace behind."

"All men, if they work not as in the great taskmaster's eye, will work wrong, and work unhappily for themselves and for you."

"No man sees far, most see no
farther than their noses."

"He is wise who can instruct us and assist us in the business of virtuous living."

"Of all your troubles, great and small, the greatest are the ones that don't happen at all."

"To reform a world, to reform a nation, no wise man will undertake; and all but foolish men know, that the only solid, though a far slower reformation, is what each begins and perfects on himself."

"I grow daily to honour facts more and more, and theory less and less. A fact, it seems to me, is a great thing; a sentence printed, if not by God, then at least by the Devil."

"For suffering and enduring there is no remedy, but striving and doing."

"The best effect of any book is that it excites the reader to self activity."

"Men do less than they ought, unless
they do all they can."

"The Bible is the truest utterance that ever came by alphabetic letters from the soul of man, through which, as through a window divinely opened, all men can look into the stillness of eternity, and discern in glimpses their far-distant, long-forgotten home."

"There are but two ways of paying debt: Increase of industry in raising income, increase of thrift in laying out."

"Only the person of worth can recognize the worth in others."

"Of a truth, men are mystically united: a mystic bond of brotherhood makes all men one."

"Great souls are always loyally submissive, reverent to what is over them: only small mean souls are otherwise."

"No ghost was every seen by two pair of eyes."

"Humor has justly been regarded as the finest perfection of poetic genius."

"I don't pretend to understand the Universe - it's a great deal bigger than I am."

"A man cannot make a pair of shoes rightly unless he do it in a devout manner."

"If you are ever in doubt as to whether to kiss a pretty girl, always give her the benefit of the doubt."

"A man's felicity consists not in the outward and visible blessing of fortune, but in the inward and unseen perfections and riches of the mind."

"The world is a republic of mediocrities, and always was."

"Men seldom, or rather never for a
length of time and deliberately,
rebel against anything that does not
deserve rebelling against."

"Oh, give us the man who sings at his work."

"Good breeding differs, if at all,
from high breeding only as it
gracefully remembers the rights of
others, rather than gracefully insists
on its own rights."

"The tragedy of life is not so much what men suffer, but rather what they miss."

"A good book is the purest essence
of a human soul."

"Love is not altogether a Delirium," says he elsewhere; "yet has it many points in common therewith. "."

"Man is, properly speaking, based upon hope, he has no other possession but hope; this world of his is emphatically the place of hope."

"When new turns of behavior cease to appear in the life of the individual, its behavior ceases to be intelligent."

"To us also, through every star, through every blade of grass, is not God made visible if we will open our minds and our eyes."

"The only happiness a brave person ever troubles themselves in asking about, is happiness enough to get their work done."

"Not what I have, but what I do is my kingdom."

"Man's unhappiness, as I construe, comes of his greatness; it is because there is an Infinite in him, which with all his cunning he cannot quite bury under the Finite."

"All work, even cotton-spinning, is noble; work is alone noble."

"The fearful unbelief is unbelief in yourself."

"No amount of ability is of the slightest avail without honor."

"All great peoples are conservative."

"No sadder proof can be given by a man of his own littleness than disbelief in great men."

"Clever men are good, but they are
not the best."

"The work an unknown good man has done is like a vein of water flowing hidden underground, secretly making the ground green."

"Genius is an infinite capacity for taking pains."

"In the long-run every Government is the exact symbol of its People, with their wisdom and unwisdom; we have to say, Like People like Government."

"Show me the person you honor, for I know better by that the kind of person you are. For you show me what your idea of humanity is."

"No man who has once heartily and wholly laughed can be altogether irreclaimably bad."

"I don't like to talk much with people who always agree with me. It is amusing to coquette with an echo for a little while, but one soon tires of it."

"Love is the only game that is not called on account of darkness."

"No nobler feeling than this, of admiration for one higher than himself, dwells in the breast of man. It is to this hour, and at all hours, the vivifying influence in man's life."

"Even in the meanest sorts of labor, the whole soul of a man is composed into a kind of real harmony the instant he sets himself to work."

"Speech is of time, silence is of
eternity."

"If time is precious, no book that will not improve by repeated readings deserves to be read at all."

"One life; a little gleam of Time between two Eternities; no second chance to us for evermore!"

"Fame, we may understand, is no sure test of merit, but only a probability of such: it is an accident, not a property, of a man; like light, it can give little or nothing, but at most may show what is given."

"That there should one man die ignorant who had capacity for knowledge, this I call a tragedy."

"Biography is the only true history."

"Thought once awakened does not again slumber; unfolds itself into a System of Thought; grows, in man after man, generation after generation, - till its full stature is reached, and such System of Thought can grow no farther, but must give place to another."

"Eternity looks grander and kinder if time grow meaner and more hostile."

"A sad spectacle. If they be inhabited, what a scope for misery and folly. If they be not inhabited, what a waste of space."

"Ill-health, of body or of mind, is defeat. Health alone is victory. Let all men, if they can manage it, contrive to be healthy!"

"Fame, we may understand, is no sure test of merit, but only a probability of such; it is an accident, not a property of man."

"Painful for a person is rebellious independence, only in loving companionship with his associates does a person feel safe: Only in reverently bowing down before the higher does a person feel exalted."

"My whinstone house my castle is, I have my own four walls."

"Great is journalism. Is not every able editor a ruler of the world, being the persuader of it?"

"France was long a despotism tempered by epigrams."

"Midas-eared Mammonism, double-barrelled Dilettantism, and their thousand adjuncts and corollaries, are not the Law by which God Almighty has appointed this His universe to go."

"Out of Eternity the new day is born; Into Eternity at night will return."

"Conclusive facts are inseparable from inconclusive except by a head that already understands and knows."

"Courtesy is the due of man to man; not of suit-of-clothes to suit-of-clothes."

"Debt is a bottomless sea."

"The past is always attractive
because it is drained of fear."

"Blessed is he who has found his work; let him ask no other blessedness. He has a work, a life-purpose; he has found it, and will follow it! How, as a free-flowing channel, dug and torn by noble force through the sour mudswamp of one's existence, like an ever-deepening river there, it runs and flows."

"We have not the love of greatness, but the love of the love of greatness."

"A person with half volition goes backwards and forwards, but makes no progress on even the smoothest of roads."

"A man's religion consists, not of the many things he is in doubt of and tries to believe, but of the few he is assured of and has no need of effort for believing."

"Give us, O give us the man who sings at his work! Be his occupation what it may, he is equal to any of those who follow the same pursuit in silent sullenness. He will do more in the same time . he will do it better . he will persevere longer. One is scarcely sensible to fatigue while he marches to music. The very stars are said to make harmony as they revolve in their spheres."

"The first purpose of clothes. was not warmth or decency, but ornament. Among wild people, we find tattooing and painting even prior to clothes. The first spiritual want of a barbarous man is decoration; as indeed we still see among the barbarous classes in civilized countries."

"For man is not the creature and product of Mechanism; but, in a far truer sense, its creator and producer."

"Every noble crown is, and on Earth will forever be, a crown of thorns."

"A thought once awakened does not again slumber."

"I think Scandinavian Paganism, to us here, is more interesting than any other. It is, for one thing, the latest; it continued in these regions of Europe till the eleventh century; 800 years ago the Norwegians were still worshipers of Odin. It is interesting also as the creed of our fathers; the men whose blood still runs in our veins, whom doubtless we still resemble in so many ways."

"Who is there that, in logical words, can express the effect music has on us?"

"This London City, with all of its houses, palaces, steam-engines, cathedrals, and huge immeasurable traffic an tumult, what is it but a Thought, but millions of Thoughts made into One-a huge immeasurable Spirit of a Thought, embodied in brick, in iron, smoke, dust, Palaces, Parliaments, Hackney Coaches, Katherine Docks, and the rest of it! Not a brick was made but some man had to think of the making of that brick."

"The world is a thing that a man must learn to despise, and even to neglect, before he can learn to reverence it, and work in it and for it."

"In our wide world there is but one altogether fatal personage, the dunce,-he that speaks irrationally, that sees not, and yet thinks he sees."

"A man protesting against error is on the way towards uniting himself with all men that believe in truth."

"Faith is loyalty to some inspired teacher, some spiritual hero."

"Unity, agreement, is always silent or soft-voiced; it is only discord that loudly proclaims itself."

"Man always worships something; always he sees the Infinite shadowed forth in something finite; and indeed can and must so see it in any finite thing, once tempt him well to fix his eyes thereon."

"A man with a half volition goes backwards and forwards, and makes no way on the smoothest road; a man with a whole volition advances on the roughest, and will reach his purpose, if there be even a little worthiness in it. The man without a purpose is like a ship without a rudder - a waif, a nothing, a no man. Have a purpose in life and having it, throw such strength of mind and muscle into your work as God has given you."

"There are remedies for all things
but death."

"There is a majesty and mystery in nature, take her as you will. The essence of poetry comes breathing to a mind that feels from every province of her empire."

"The leafy blossoming present time springs from the whole past, remembered and unrememberable."

"Insurrection, never so necessary, is a most sad necessity; and governors who wait for that to instruct them are surely getting into the fatalest course."

"There is no heroic poem in the world but is at bottom a biography, the life of a man."

"No man is born without ambitious worldly desires."

"I want to meet my God awake."

"Evil and good are everywhere, like shadow and substance; inseparable (for men) yet not hostile, only opposed."

"Evil, once manfully fronted, ceases to be evil; there is generous battle-hope in place of dead, passive misery; the evil itself has become a kind of good."

"Money will buy money's worth;
but the thing men call fame, what is
it?"

"What a wretched thing is all fame! A renown of the highest sort endures, say, for two thousand years. And then? Why, then, a fathomless eternity swallows it. Work for eternity; not the meagre rhetorical eternity of the periodical critics, but for the real eternity wherein dwelleth the Divine."

"How indestructibly the good grows, and propagates itself, even among the weedy entanglements of evil."

"Consider in fact, a body of six hundred and fifty-eight miscellaneous persons, set to consult about "business," with twenty-seven millions, mostly fools, assiduously listening to them, and checking and criticising them. Was there ever, since the world began, will there ever be till the world end, any "business" accomplished in these circumstances?"

"We observe with confidence that the truly strong mind, view it as intellect or morality, or under any other aspect, is nowise the mind acquainted with its strength; that here the sign of health is unconsciousness."

"Habit and imitation-there is nothing more perennial in us than these two. They are the source of all working, and all apprenticeship, of all practice, and all learning, in this world."

"A word spoken in season, at the right moment; is the mother of ages."

"We are to take no counsel with flesh and blood; give ear to no vain cavils, vain sorrows and wishes; to know that we know nothing, that the worst and cruelest to our eyes is not what it seems, that we have to receive whatsoever befalls us as sent from God above, and say, "It is good and wise,-God is great! Though He slay me, yet I trust in Him. " Islam means, in its way, denial of self. This is yet the highest wisdom that heaven has revealed to our earth."

"If I say that Shakespeare is the greatest of intellects, I have said all concerning him. But there is more in Shakespeare's intellect than we have yet seen. It is what I call an unconscious intellect; there is more virtue in it that he himself is aware of."

"He who cannot withal keep his mind to himself cannot practice any considerable thing whatsoever."

"Not one false man but doth
uncountable evil."

"The true epic of our times is not "Arm's and the Man," but "Tools and the Man"-an infinitely wider kind of epic."

"All true work is sacred."

"Labor is life: from the inmost heart of the worker rises his God-given force, the sacred celestial life-essence breathed into him by Almighty God!"

"Labor, wide as the earth, has its summit in heaven."

"Nature admits no lie."

"Nakedness, hunger, distress of all kinds, death itself have been cheerfully suffered, when the heart was right. It is the feeling of injustice that is insupportable to all men."

"Without oblivion, there is no remembrance possible. When both oblivion and memory are wise, when the general soul of man is clear, melodious, true, there may come a modern Iliad as memorial of the Past."

"The sincere alone can recognize sincerity."

"Piety does not mean that a man should make a sour face about things, and refuse to enjoy in moderation what his Maker has given."

"Learn to be good readers, which is perhaps a more difficult thing than you imagine. Learn to be discriminative in your reading; to read faithfully, and with your best attention, all kinds of things which you have a real interest in,-a real, not an imaginary,-and which you find to be really fit for what you are engaged in."

"An everlasting lodestar, that beams the brighter in the heavens the darker here on earth grows the night."

"If there be not a religious element in the relations of men, such relations are miserable and doomed to ruin."

"The goal of yesterday will be our starting-point to-morrow."

"No mortal has a right to wag his tongue, much less to wag his pen, without saying something."

"Whose school-hours are all the days and nights of our existence."

"What are your historical Facts still more your biographical Wilt thou know a man by stringing-together beadrolls of what thou namest Facts."

"At the bottom there is no perfect history; there is none such conceivable. All past centuries have rotted down, and gone confusedly dumb and quiet."

"Happy season of virtuous youth, when shame is still an impassable barrier, and the sacred air-cities of hope have not shrunk into the mean clay hamlets of reality; and man, by his nature, is yet infinite and free."

"A dandy is a clothes-wearing man-a man whose trade, office, and existence consist in the wearing of clothes. Every faculty of his soul, spirit, person and purse is heroically consecrated to this one object-the wearing of clothes, wisely and well; so that, as others dress to live, he lives to dress."

"Democracy will itself accomplish the salutary universal change from delusive to real, and make a new blessed world of us by and by."

"The choking, sweltering, deadly, and killing rule of no rule; the consecration of cupidity and braying of folly, and dim stupidity and baseness, in most of the affairs of men. Slopshirts attainable three-halfpence cheaper by the ruin of living bodies and immortal souls."

"Earnestness alone makes life eternity."

"Friend, hast thou considered the "rugged, all-nourishing earth," as Sophocles well names her; how she feeds the sparrow on the housetop, much more her darling man?"

"Neither in tailoring nor in legislating does man proceed by mere accident."

"We arc the miracle of miracles, the great inscrutable mystery of God."

"For every one hundred men who can stand adversity there is only one who can withstand prosperity."

"Wondrous is the strength of cheerfulness, altogether past calculation its powers of endurance."

"Happy season of childhood! Kind Nature, that art to all a bountiful mother; that visitest the poor man's hut With auroral radiance; and for thy nursling hast provided a soft swathing of love and infinite hope wherein he waxes and slumbers, danced round by sweetest dreams!"

"It is a fact which escapes no one, that, generally speaking, whoso is acquainted with his worth has but a little stock to cultivate acquaintance with."

"To say that we have a clear conscience is to utter a solecism; had we never sinned we should have had no conscience. Were defeat unknown, neither would victory be celebrated by songs of triumph."

"What the light of your mind, which is the direct inspiration of the Almighty, pronounces incredible, that, in God's name, leave uncredited. At your peril do not try believing that!"

"The great law of culture is, Let each become all that he was created capable of being; expand, if possible, to his full growth; resisting all impediments, casting off all foreign, especially all noxious adhesions, and show himself at length in his own shape and stature be these what they may."

"A man-be the heavens ever praised!-is sufficient for himself."

"It is not to taste sweet things; but to do noble and true things, and vindicate himself under God's heaven as a God-made man, that the poorest son of Adam dimly longs. Show him the way of doing that, the dullest day-drudge kindles into a hero. They wrong man greatly who say he is to be seduced by ease. Difficulty, abnegation, martyrdom, death, are the allurements that act on the heart of man. Kindle the inner genial life of him, you have a flame that burns up all lower considerations."

"Good Christian people, here lies for you an inestimable loan; take all heed thereof, in all carefulness, employ it: with high recompense, or else with heavy penalty, will it one day be required back."

"Rare benevolence, the minister of God."

"The true eye for talent presupposes the true reverence for it."

"Taste, if it mean anything but a paltry connoisseurship, must mean a general susceptibility to truth and nobleness, a sense to discern, and a heart to love and reverence all beauty, order, goodness, wheresoever, or in whatsoever forms and accompaniments they are to be seen. This surely implies, as its chief condition, not any given external rank or situation, but a finely-gifted mind, purified into harmony with itself, into keenness and justness of vision; above all, kindled into love and generous admiration."

"He who talks much about virtue in the abstract, begins to be suspected; it is shrewdly guessed that where there is great preaching there will be little almsgiving."

"The modern majesty consists in work. What a man can do is his greatest ornament, and he always consults his dignity by doing it."

"The deepest depth of vulgarism is that of setting up money as the ark of the covenant."

"Goethe's devil is a cultivated personage and acquainted with the modern sciences; sneers at witchcraft and the black art even while employing them, and doubts most things, nay, half disbelieves even his own existence."

"The nobleness of silence. The highest melody dwells only in silence,-the sphere melody, the melody of health."

"Well might the ancients make silence a god; for it is the element of all godhood, infinitude, or transcendental greatness,-at once the source and the ocean wherein all such begins and ends."

"Alas! while the body stands so broad and brawny, must the soul lie blinded, dwarfed, stupefied, almost annihilated? Alas! this was, too, a breath of God, bestowed in heaven, but on earth never to be unfolded!"

"Speech that leads not to action, still
more that hinders it, is a nuisance
on the earth."

"I grow daily to honor facts more and more, and theory less and less."

"They only are wise who know that they know nothing."

"Man makes circumstances, and spiritually as well as economically, is the artificer of his own fortune."

"A fair day's wages for a fair day's work."

"All evil is like a nightmare; the instant you stir under it, the evil is gone."

"Stern accuracy in inquiring, bold imagination in describing, these are the cogs on which history soars or flutters and wobbles."

"Not our Logical, Mensurative faculty, but our Imaginative one is King over us; I might say, Priest and Prophet to lead us heavenward; or Magician and Wizard to lead us hellward."

"We call that fire of the black thunder-cloud "electricity," and lecture learnedly about it, and grind the like of it out of glass and silk: but what is it? What made it? Whence comes it? Whither goes it?"

"Know what thou canst work at,
and work at it like a Hercules."

"There is but one thing without honor, smitten with eternal barrenness, inability to do or to be,-insincerity, unbelief."

"Trust not the heart of that man for whom old clothes are not venerable."

"The greatest mistake is to imagine
that we never err."

"The barrenest of all mortals is the sentimentalist."

"The king is the man who can."

"Habit is the deepest law of human nature."

"What an enormous magnifier is tradition! How a thing grows in the human memory and in the human imagination, when love, worship, and all that lies in the human heart, is there to encourage it."

"There is a perennial nobleness, and even sacredness, in work. Were he never so benighted, forgetful of his high calling, there is always hope in a man that actually and earnestly works: in idleness alone there is perpetual despair."

"The purpose of man is in action
not thought."

"A man perfects himself by working. Foul jungles are cleared away, fair seed-fields rise instead, and stately cities; and with the man himself first ceases to be a jungle, and foul unwholesome desert thereby. The man is now a man."

"Histories are a kind of distilled newspapers."

"Is man's civilization only a wrappage, through which the savage nature of him can still burst, infernal as ever?"

"Skepticism . is not intellectual only
it is moral also, a chronic atrophy
and disease of the whole soul."

"Genius' which means transcendent capacity of taking trouble, first of all."

"A judicious man looks at Statistics, not to "get knowledge, but to save himself from having ignorance foisted 'on him"."

"Democracy is, by the nature of it, a self-canceling business: and gives in the long run a net result of zero."

"Intellect is the soul of man, the only immortal part of him."

"O Heaven, it is mysterious, it is awful to consider that we not only carry each a future Ghost within him; but are, in very deed, Ghosts!"

"Action hangs, as it were, dissolved in speech, in thoughts whereof speech is the shadow; and precipitates itself therefrom. The kind of speech in a man betokens the kind of action you will get from him."

"Happy the People whose Annals
are blank in History Books!"

"No conquest can ever become permanent which does not show itself beneficial to the conquered as well as to the conquerors."

"If you are looking at data over and over you better be taking away valuable insight every time. If you are constantly looking at data that isn't leading to strategic action stop wasting your time and look for more Actionable Analytics."

"Infinite is the help man can yield to man."

"Men's hearts ought not to be set against one another, but set with one another and all against evil only."

"But the whim we have of happiness is somewhat thus. By certain valuations, and averages, of our own striking, we come upon some sort of average terrestrial lot; this we fancy belongs to us by nature, and of indefeasible rights. It is simple payment of our wages, of our deserts; requires neither thanks nor complaint. Foolish soul! What act of legislature was there that thou shouldst be happy? A little while ago thou hadst no right to be at all."

"History is a great dust heap."

"Also, what mountains of dead ashes, wreck and burnt bones, does assiduous pedantry dig up from the past time and name it History."

"Pain was not given thee merely to be miserable under; learn from it, turn it to account."

"We have not read an author till we have seen his object, whatever it may be, as he saw it."

"The merit of originality is not novelty; it is sincerity. The believing man is the original man; whatsoever he believes, he believes it for himself, not for another."

"Laws, written, if not on stone tables, yet on the azure of infinitude, in the inner heart of God's creation, certain as life, certain as death, are there, and thou shalt not disobey them."

"Rest is for the dead."

"Burke said there were Three Estates in Parliament; but, in the Reporter's gallery yonder, there sat a fourth estate more important far than they all."

"Have not I myself known five hundred living soldiers sabred into crows' meat for a piece of glazed cotton, which they call their flag; which had you sold it at any market-cross, would not have brought above three groschen?"

"Skepticism, as I said, is not intellectual only; it is moral also; a chronic atrophy and disease of the whole soul. A man lives by believing something; not by debating and arguing about many things. A sad case for him when all that he can manage to believe is something he can button in his pocket, and with one or the other organ eat and digest! Lower than that he will not get."

"The hell of these days is the fear of not getting along, especially of not making money."

"Scarcely two hundred years back can Fame recollect articulately at all; and there she but maunders and mumbles."

"This is the eternal law of Nature for a man, my beneficent Exeter-Hall friends; this, that he shall be permitted, encouraged, and if need be, compelled to do what work the Maker of him has intended by the making of him for this world! Not that he should eat pumpkin with never such felicity in the West India Islands is, or can be, the blessedness of our Black friend; but that he should do useful work there, according as the gifts have been bestowed on him for that."

"To the mean eye all things are trivial, as certainly as to the jaundiced they are yellow."

"There is no permanent place in this universe for evil. Evil may hide behind this fallacy and that, but it will be hunted from fallacy to fallacy until there is no more fallacy for it to hide behind."

"I should say sincerity, a deep, great, genuine sincerity, is the first characteristic of all men in any way heroic."

"There is always hope in a man that actually and earnestly works: in Idleness alone is there perpetual despair."

"Innumerable are the illusions and legerdemain-tricks of custom: but of all of these, perhaps the cleverest is her knack of persuading us that the miraculous, by simple repetition, ceases to be miraculous."

"A man lives by believing
something."

"Dinners are defined as 'the ultimate act of communion;' men that can have communion in nothing else, can sympathetically eat together, can still rise into some glow of brotherhood over food and wine."

"At worst, is not this an unjust world, full of nothing but beasts of prey, four-footed or two-footed?"

"So here hath been dawning Another blue day; Think, wilt thou let it Slip useless away? Out of eternity This new day is born, Into eternity At night will return."

"Pin thy faith to no man's sleeve.
Hast thou not two eyes of thy own?"

"It is well said, in every sense, that a man's religion is the chief fact with regard to him."

"Fire is the best of servants, but what a master!"

"Do nothing, only keep agitating, debating; and things will destroy themselves."

"Work earnestly at anything, you will by degrees learn to work at all things."

"Genuine Work alone, what thou workest faithfully, that is eternal, as the Almighty Founder and World-Builder himself."

"If those gentlemen would let me alone I should be much obliged to them. I would say, as Shakespeare would say. Sweet Friend, for Jesus sake forbear."

"No sooner does a great man depart, and leave his character as public property, than a crowd of little men rushes towards it. There they are gathered together, blinking up to it with such vision as they have, scanning it from afar, hovering round it this way and that, each cunningly endeavoring, by all arts, to catch some reflex of it in the little mirror of himself."

"Language is called the garment of thought: however, it should rather be, language is the flesh-garment, the body, of thought."

"A Fourth Estate, of Able Editors, springs up."

"And yet without labour there were no ease, no rest, so much as conceivable."

"There is endless merit in a man's knowing when to have done."

"The stifled hum of midnight, when traffic has lain down to rest, and the chariot wheels of Vanity, still rolling here and there through distant streets, are bearing her to halls roofed in and lighted to the due pitch for her; and only vice and misery, to prowl or to moan like night birds, are abroad."

"Before philosophy can teach by Experience, the Philosophy has to be in readiness, the Experience must be gathered and intelligibly recorded."

"He who first shortened the labor of Copyists by device of Movable Types was disbanding hired armies and cashiering most Kings and Senates, and creating a whole new Democratic world: he had invented the Art of printing."

"Skepticism means, not intellectual doubt alone, but moral doubt."

"Histories are as perfect as the Historian is wise, and is gifted with an eye and a soul."

"History: A distillation of rumor."

"All history . is an inarticulate Bible."

"Be a pattern to others, and then all will go well; for as a whole city is affected by the licentious passions and vices of great men, so it is likewise reformed by their moderation."

"The archenemy is the arch stupid!"

"Of all the things which man can do or make here below, by far the most momentous, wonderful, and worthy are the things we call books."

"Force, force, everywhere force; we ourselves a mysterious force in the centre of that. "There is not a leaf rotting on the highway but has Force in it: how else could it rot?" [As used in his time, by the word force, Carlyle means energy.]."

"Tobacco smoke is the one element in which, by our European manners, men can sit silent together without embarrassment, and where no man is bound to speak one word more than he has actually and veritably got to say. Nay, rather every man is admonished and enjoined by the laws of honor, and even of personal ease, to stop short of that point; and at all events to hold his peace and take to his pipe again the instant he has spoken his meaning, if he chance to have any."

"Life is a series of lessons that have to be understood."

"All destruction, by violent revolution or however it be, is but new creation on a wider scale."

"Enjoying things which are pleasant; that is not the evil; it is the reducing of our moral self to slavery by them that is."

"To know, to get into the truth of anything, is ever a mystic art, of which the best logic's can but babble on the surface."

"The authentic insight and experience of any human soul, were it but insight and experience in hewing of wood and drawing of water, is real knowledge, a real possession and acquirement."

"The universe is but one vast Symbol of God."

"When Pococke inquired of Grotius, where the proof was of that story of the pigeon, trained to pick peas from Mahomet's (Muhammad's) ear, and pass for an angel dictating to him? Grotius answered that there was no proof!"

"If Hero means sincere man, why may not every one of us be a Hero?"

"If a book comes from the heart, it will contrive to reach other hearts; all art and author-craft are of small amount to that."

"Dishonesty is the raw material not of quacks only, but also in great part dupes."

"The whole past is the procession of the present."

"Statistics, one may hope, will improve gradually, and become good for something. Meanwhile, it is to be feared the crabbed satirist was partly right, as things go: "A judicious man," says he, "looks at Statistics, not to get knowledge, but to save himself from having ignorance foisted on him. "."

"The condition of the most passionate enthusiast is to be preferred over the individual who, because of the fear of making a mistake, won't in the end affirm or deny anything."

"The lightning spark of thought generated in the solitary mind awakens its likeness in another mind."

"The first sin in our universe was Lucifer's self conceit."

"In every object there is inexhaustible meaning; the eye sees in it what the eye brings means of seeing."

"For, strictly considered, what is all Knowledge too but recorded Experience, and a product of History; of which, therefore, Reasoning and Belief, no less than Action and Passion, are essential materials?"

"Experience takes dreadfully high school-wages, but he teaches like no other."

"The Present is the living sum-total of the whole Past."

"Love is ever the beginning of knowledge as fire is of light."

"In this world there is one godlike thing, the essence of all that was or ever will be of godlike in this world: the veneration done to Human Worth by the hearts of men."

"The crash of the whole solar and stellar systems could only kill you once."

"The past is all holy to us; the dead are all holy; even they that were wicked when alive."

"Variety is the condition of harmony."

"Virtue is like health: the harmony of the whole man."

"The end of Man is an Action, and not a Thought, though it were the noblest?"

"This world, after all our science and sciences, is still a miracle; wonderful, inscrutable, magical and more, to whosoever will think of it."

"The true past departs not, no truth or goodness realized by man ever dies, or can die; but all is still here, and, recognized or not, lives and works through endless change."

"O poor mortals, how ye make this earth bitter for each other."

"Nine-tenths of the miseries and vices of mankind proceed from idleness."

"Conviction never so excellent, is worthless until it coverts itself into conduct."

"He who could foresee affairs three days in advance would be rich for thousands of years."

"No person is important enough to make me angry."

"If what you have done is unjust,
you have not succeeded."

"Culture is the process by which a person becomes all that they were created capable of being."

"It is a vain hope to make people happy by politics."

"Reform is not pleasant, but grievous; no person can reform themselves without suffering and hard work, how much less a nation."

"Not brute force but only persuasion and faith are the kings of this world."

"There is a great discovery still to be made in literature, that of paying literary men by the quantity they do not write."

"The cut of a garment speaks of intellect and talent and the color of temperament and heart."

"The difference between Socrates and Jesus? The great conscious and the immeasurably great unconscious."

"Thought is the parent of the deed."

"Originality is a thing we constantly clamour for, and constantly quarrel with."

"Speech is human, silence is divine, yet also brutish and dead: therefore we must learn both arts."

"Nothing that was worthy in the past departs; no truth or goodness realized by man ever dies, or can die."

"Wonder is the basis of worship."

"If an eloquent speaker speak not the truth, is there a more horrid kind of object in creation?"

"In books lies the soul of the whole Past Time; the articulate audible voice of the Past, when the body and material substance of it has altogether vanished like a dream."

"The word of Mohammad is a voice direct from nature's own heart - all else is wind in comparison."

"Look to be treated by others as you have treated others."

"The outer passes away; the innermost is the same yesterday, today, and forever."

"Writing is a dreadful labor, yet not so dreadful as Idleness."

"Narrative is linear, but action has breadth and depth as well as height and is solid."

"No violent extreme endures."

"Imagination is a poor matter when it has to part company with understanding."

"The courage we desire and prize is not the courage to die decently, but to live manfully."

"The actual well seen is ideal."

"Let him who would move and convince others, be first moved and convinced himself."

"The greatest event for the world is the arrival of a new and wise person."

"Rich as we are in biography, a well-written life is almost as rare as a well-spent one; and there are certainly many more men whose history deserves to be recorded than persons willing and able to record it."

"No age seemed the age of romance to itself."

"With stupidity and sound digestion, man may front much."